The Balancing Act: Individual Rights, Privacy, and National Security

Copyright Page

TITLE: The Balancing Act: Individual Rights, Privacy, and National Security

1ST Edition

ISBN: 9798223748786

The Balancing Act: Individual Rights, Privacy, and National Security

By Roberto Miguel Rodriguez

Chapter 1: Introduction

Background and Context

In the digital age, the delicate balance between individual rights, privacy, and national security has become increasingly complex. As technology advances at an unprecedented pace, governments around the world have sought to enhance their surveillance capabilities in order to combat evolving threats to national security. However, this expansion of surveillance measures has raised significant concerns among civil liberties advocates and privacy-conscious individuals.

"The Balancing Act: Individual Rights, Privacy, and National Security" delves into the heart of this pressing issue, shedding light on the potential infringement on individual rights and privacy resulting from the Act's surveillance measures. This subchapter aims to provide scholars, professors, students, politicians, and legislators with essential background information and contextual understanding necessary to engage in critical discussions surrounding civil liberties and privacy concerns.

The chapter begins by examining the historical context that has contributed to the current debate. It delves into landmark cases and pivotal events that have shaped the legal framework pertaining to individual rights and privacy. By exploring key court decisions, such as the Fourth Amendment in the United States or the European Convention on Human Rights, the subchapter establishes a foundation for comprehending the legal complexities inherent in the balancing act between individual rights and national security.

Furthermore, the subchapter highlights the rapid advancements in technology that have fueled the expansion of surveillance capabilities. It explores the advent of the internet, social media platforms, and the proliferation of personal data, illustrating how these developments have created new challenges when safeguarding individual privacy. Additionally, it delves into the emergence of sophisticated surveillance technologies, such as facial recognition systems and artificial intelligence, which further complicate the delicate balance.

To offer a comprehensive view, the subchapter analyzes the legislative landscape surrounding surveillance measures in various countries. It examines the differences and similarities in legal frameworks, as well as the varying levels of oversight and accountability imposed on surveillance agencies. By comparing different approaches, readers gain a global perspective on the challenges faced by policymakers when attempting to strike the right balance between security concerns and individual rights.

Through a thorough exploration of historical, legal, and technological perspectives, this subchapter sets the stage for a deeper understanding of the civil liberties and privacy concerns that arise from the Act's surveillance measures. By equipping scholars, professors, students, politicians, and legislators with the necessary background and context, "The Balancing Act" aims to foster informed discussions and facilitate the development of balanced and effective policies that protect both national security and individual rights.

Purpose and Scope

In today's interconnected world, the delicate balance between individual rights, privacy, and national security has become a paramount concern. As we strive to protect our nations from evolving threats, it is essential to examine the potential infringement on individual rights and privacy caused by surveillance measures. This subchapter, titled "Purpose and Scope," serves as a critical introduction to the book "The Balancing Act: Individual Rights, Privacy, and National Security," catering to scholars, professors, students, politicians, legislators, and those interested in civil liberties and privacy concerns.

The primary purpose of this subchapter is to provide a comprehensive overview of the book's central theme and lay the groundwork for subsequent discussions. It aims to initiate a thoughtful and informed conversation about the complex interplay between individual rights, privacy, and national security. By exploring the potential tensions between these elements, we can better understand the challenges faced by policymakers, lawmakers, and society at large.

Within this subchapter, readers will find an exploration of the purpose and scope of the book, delving into the multifaceted issues surrounding civil liberties and privacy concerns. We will examine the potential consequences of surveillance measures on individual rights, exploring the ethical, legal, and societal implications of such actions. Through a systematic and interdisciplinary approach, we will dissect the various perspectives and arguments surrounding these contentious issues.

Moreover, this subchapter will introduce the key stakeholders involved in the discourse. Scholars, professors, students, politicians, and legislators are invited to engage in an intellectual dialogue that transcends personal beliefs and political affiliations. By fostering collaboration across diverse fields and perspectives, we aim to develop a comprehensive understanding of the challenges and potential solutions that lie ahead.

Finally, this subchapter will provide a roadmap for the subsequent chapters in the book. It will offer a glimpse into the topics to be covered, such as the legal framework surrounding surveillance measures, technological advancements and their impact on privacy, and case studies examining real-world implications.

"The Balancing Act: Individual Rights, Privacy, and National Security" holds the potential to shape the discourse on civil liberties and privacy concerns. By addressing the purpose and scope of this book, we hope to empower scholars, professors, students, politicians, and legislators to critically analyze the intricate relationship between individual rights, privacy, and national security. Through informed discussions and rigorous analysis, we can strive for a balanced approach that safeguards both our individual freedoms and collective security.

Research Questions

In this subchapter, we will delve into the fundamental research questions surrounding the delicate balance between individual rights, privacy, and national security as explored in the book "The Balancing Act: Individual Rights, Privacy, and National Security." Aimed at scholars, professors, students, politicians, and legislators, this section will address civil liberties and privacy concerns, specifically examining the potential infringement on individual rights and privacy resulting from the Act's surveillance measures. Through rigorous inquiry and critical analysis, we will explore the complex dimensions of this ongoing debate.

1. What are the key elements of the Act's surveillance measures and how do they intersect with civil liberties and privacy rights?

This question aims to provide a comprehensive understanding of the surveillance measures outlined in the Act. By examining the Act's provisions, we will analyze the potential impact on civil liberties and privacy rights, including the collection and analysis of personal data, monitoring of communication channels, and the use of advanced technologies in surveillance.

2. To what extent do the Act's surveillance measures infringe upon individual rights and privacy?

This question seeks to evaluate the balance between national security imperatives and the protection of individual rights. Through a thorough examination of case studies and legal frameworks, we will critically assess the potential infringement on privacy rights and individual freedoms caused by the Act's surveillance measures.

3. How do civil liberties and privacy concerns impact public trust in government and security agencies?

This question delves into the broader societal implications of the Act's surveillance measures. By analyzing public opinion surveys, media coverage, and historical examples, we will explore the relationship between civil liberties, privacy concerns, and public trust in government and security agencies. We will consider the potential consequences of eroded trust, such as social backlash, decreased cooperation with authorities, and possible threats to national security.

4. What are the viable alternatives to balance national security with individual rights and privacy?

This question aims to identify potential alternatives and policy recommendations that strike a balance between national security imperatives and the protection of civil liberties and privacy rights. Through comparative analysis of different countries' approaches, legal frameworks, and technological solutions, we will explore possibilities for safeguarding both national security and individual rights.

By addressing these research questions, this subchapter will provide scholars, professors, students, politicians, and legislators with a comprehensive understanding of the intricate relationship between individual rights, privacy, and national security. It will equip readers with the knowledge needed to critically examine the potential infringement on individual rights and privacy resulting from the Act's surveillance measures, enabling them to contribute to informed discussions, policy formulation, and the protection of civil liberties in an increasingly interconnected world.

Chapter 2: Understanding Individual Rights and Privacy

Definition and Importance of Individual Rights

In the context of "The Balancing Act: Individual Rights, Privacy, and National Security," it is imperative to explore the definition and significance of individual rights. This subchapter aims to provide scholars, professors, students, politicians, and legislators with a comprehensive understanding of the concepts of individual rights, their intrinsic value, and the potential infringement on these rights due to surveillance measures implemented under the Act.

Individual rights, also known as civil liberties, are the fundamental entitlements and freedoms that every person possesses inherently by virtue of being human. These rights include but are not limited to the right to life, liberty, and security of person, freedom of speech, expression, assembly, and association, as well as the right to privacy. They form the backbone of a democratic society, ensuring that individuals are free to pursue their own interests, beliefs, and values without undue interference from the state or other individuals.

The importance of individual rights cannot be overstated. They act as a safeguard against oppression, tyranny, and the abuse of power. Individual rights empower citizens, enabling them to participate actively in the democratic process, express dissenting opinions, and hold those in authority accountable. Moreover, these rights contribute to the development of a diverse and inclusive society, fostering creativity, innovation, and progress.

However, the implementation of surveillance measures, as outlined in the Act, raises concerns about potential infringements on individual rights and privacy. It is crucial to critically examine the balance between national security imperatives and the protection of civil liberties. The subchapter will delve into the challenges posed by these surveillance measures, including the potential for unwarranted intrusion into private lives, the chilling effect on freedom of expression and association, and the erosion of trust between citizens and the state.

By addressing these concerns, scholars, professors, students, politicians, and legislators will gain a nuanced understanding of the delicate balance required between individual rights and national security concerns. They will be equipped to evaluate the implications of the Act's surveillance measures, ensuring that any encroachments on civil liberties are justified, necessary, and proportionate. The subchapter will also offer insights into potential policy reforms and safeguards that can be implemented to strike a more effective and equitable balance between individual rights, privacy, and national security.

In conclusion, this subchapter on the definition and importance of individual rights provides a foundation for understanding the significance of civil liberties in a democratic society. It highlights the potential infringements on these rights due to surveillance measures under the Act, emphasizing the need for a thoughtful and balanced approach to ensure the protection of individual rights, privacy, and national security.

Definition and Importance of Privacy

Privacy is a fundamental human right that forms the cornerstone of our individual liberties and autonomy. It encompasses the ability to control our personal information, decisions, and activities, ensuring that we have the freedom to live our lives without unwarranted intrusion. In the context of civil liberties and privacy concerns, understanding the definition and importance of privacy is crucial to comprehending the potential infringement on individual rights and privacy resulting from surveillance measures.

Privacy can be defined as the right to be left alone, the right to control one's personal information, and the right to maintain confidentiality in various aspects of life. It extends beyond physical spaces to encompass digital privacy, which refers to the protection of personal data and online activities. In an era dominated by technology and interconnectedness, the need to safeguard privacy becomes even more critical.

The importance of privacy cannot be overstated. It allows individuals to form their own identities, make personal choices, and develop intimate relationships free from unwarranted scrutiny. Privacy also fosters trust and confidentiality, enabling individuals to share sensitive information with healthcare providers, lawyers, or counselors without fear of judgment or exposure. Furthermore, privacy serves as a necessary condition for free speech, as individuals are more likely to express themselves honestly and openly when they have the assurance that their thoughts and opinions will not be used against them.

In the context of civil liberties and privacy concerns, the potential infringement on individual rights and privacy resulting from surveillance measures must be critically examined. The balance between national security and individual privacy is a delicate one, and it is important to assess the impact of surveillance measures on civil liberties. While ensuring national security is essential, it should not come at the expense of sacrificing privacy and individual rights.

This subchapter aims to explore the multifaceted nature of privacy and its significance in the face of surveillance measures. It will delve into the ethical and legal implications of surveillance, the potential chilling effect on freedom of expression, and the erosion of trust between citizens and the state. It will also examine the importance of striking a balance between national security and privacy concerns, highlighting the need for robust oversight mechanisms and accountability.

Scholars, professors, students, politicians, and legislators will find this subchapter invaluable in their quest to understand the intricate relationship between individual rights, privacy, and national security. By critically examining the definition and importance of privacy, we can foster a more informed and nuanced discussion on how to reconcile the competing interests of security and privacy in a democratic society.

Relationship between Individual Rights and Privacy

In today's digital age, where technology has pervaded every aspect of our lives, the relationship between individual rights and privacy has become increasingly complex. This subchapter aims to explore the delicate balancing act that exists between safeguarding individual rights and protecting national security. Addressed to scholars, professors, students, politicians, and legislators, we delve into the realm of civil liberties and privacy concerns, examining the potential infringement on individual rights and privacy as a result of the Act's surveillance measures.

Privacy, a fundamental human right, forms the bedrock of a democratic society. It grants individuals the freedom to express themselves, associate with others, and maintain autonomy over their personal data. However, in the face of evolving national security threats, governments are compelled to adopt surveillance measures to protect their citizens. This necessitates a careful evaluation of the extent to which individual privacy can be compromised without jeopardizing civil liberties.

One major concern surrounding the relationship between individual rights and privacy is the potential for overreach by intelligence agencies. The Act's surveillance measures, although well-intentioned, may inadvertently infringe upon the privacy of individuals who are not suspected of any wrongdoing. Scholars and politicians must critically evaluate the balance between security and privacy, ensuring that surveillance measures are proportionate, necessary, and subject to robust oversight.

Moreover, the ubiquitous nature of technology has magnified privacy concerns. With the exponential growth of data collection, storage, and analysis, individuals are increasingly vulnerable to breaches and abuse. The subchapter explores the ethical implications of mass surveillance programs, the potential for discrimination or profiling, and the chilling effect on freedom of speech and association.

To maintain a healthy democracy, it is imperative that policymakers and legislators engage in a nuanced discussion on striking the right balance between individual rights and privacy. This subchapter serves as a platform for scholars, professors, students, and politicians to critically analyze the potential infringement on civil liberties resulting from the Act's surveillance measures. By fostering an informed debate, we can ensure the protection of individual rights while safeguarding national security.

In conclusion, the relationship between individual rights and privacy is a complex and dynamic one. The subchapter titled "Relationship between Individual Rights and Privacy" delves into the realm of civil liberties and privacy concerns, examining the potential infringement on individual rights and privacy as a result of the Act's surveillance measures. By addressing the concerns of scholars, professors, students, politicians, and legislators, we aim to foster an informed discussion on striking the delicate balance between safeguarding individual rights and protecting national security. Through this exploration, we can work towards a society that upholds privacy as a fundamental human right while ensuring the safety and well-being of its citizens.

Historical Perspectives on Individual Rights and Privacy

Throughout history, the concept of individual rights and privacy has been at the forefront of societal and political debates. This subchapter delves into the historical perspectives surrounding these fundamental principles, exploring how they have evolved and shaped our understanding of civil liberties and privacy concerns.

From ancient civilizations to modern nation-states, the struggle to strike a balance between individual rights and collective security has been a recurring theme. In ancient Athens, for instance, citizens enjoyed certain rights and protections, including the right to a fair trial, while also being subject to surveillance by the state. This tension between personal freedom and the need for security has persisted over time and is still debated today.

The Enlightenment period of the 18th century witnessed a significant shift in the understanding of individual rights and privacy. Thinkers such as John Locke and Thomas Jefferson emphasized the natural rights of individuals, which included the right to life, liberty, and property. These ideas laid the foundation for modern democratic societies, where the protection of individual rights and privacy became essential to limit the power of the state.

The challenges posed by technological advancements have further complicated the discussion on individual rights and privacy. The invention of the telegraph, telephone, and later the internet, revolutionized communication but also raised concerns about the potential intrusion into private lives. The advent of mass surveillance during the two world wars and the Cold War era intensified the debate, with governments justifying the need for surveillance in the name of national security.

In recent years, the exponential growth of digital technologies has presented new challenges to individual rights and privacy. The rise of social media platforms, data collection, and surveillance technologies has sparked concerns about the erosion of privacy and the potential abuse of personal information.

This subchapter explores these historical perspectives to provide a comprehensive understanding of the ongoing debate surrounding individual rights and privacy. It aims to equip scholars, professors, students, politicians, and legislators with the knowledge and tools necessary to critically examine the potential infringement on individual rights and privacy resulting from the Act's surveillance measures.

By delving into the past, we can better understand the present and navigate the complexities of balancing individual rights, privacy concerns, and national security in an increasingly interconnected world.

Chapter 3: Introduction to National Security Measures

Definition and Importance of National Security

National security is a multifaceted concept that encompasses the protection and preservation of a nation's interests, values, and sovereignty. It involves safeguarding a nation from external threats, such as terrorism, espionage, and military aggression, as well as internal threats like political instability, economic vulnerabilities, and social unrest. This subchapter delves into the definition and importance of national security, particularly in the context of civil liberties and privacy concerns.

In today's interconnected world, national security has become an increasingly complex issue. The rise of global terrorism, cyber warfare, and transnational crime has necessitated the development of comprehensive strategies to counter these threats effectively. It is crucial to strike a delicate balance between ensuring the safety and well-being of the nation and preserving the fundamental rights and privacy of individuals.

National security is of paramount importance as it provides the foundation for a stable and prosperous society. Without effective national security measures, a nation becomes vulnerable to various risks that can undermine its stability, economic viability, and social fabric. By safeguarding the nation's interests, national security creates an environment conducive to individual growth, economic development, and democratic governance.

However, the implementation of surveillance measures to bolster national security can potentially infringe upon individual rights and privacy. This raises concerns among civil liberties advocates, scholars, and policymakers who question the extent to which these measures should be employed. Striking the right balance between security and privacy is a delicate task that requires thoughtful consideration and robust legal and policy frameworks.

Examining the potential infringement on individual rights and privacy as a result of surveillance measures is crucial to ensure that national security efforts do not encroach upon the fundamental values of a democratic society. It is essential to assess the effectiveness and necessity of surveillance programs, the transparency and accountability of the agencies involved, and the safeguarding of individual rights in the process.

This subchapter aims to provide a comprehensive understanding of the definition and importance of national security within the context of civil liberties and privacy concerns. It explores the challenges faced in striking a balance between security and privacy and presents various perspectives from scholars, professors, students, politicians, and legislators. By engaging in this discourse, we can foster a deeper understanding of the complexities involved and work towards finding solutions that protect both national security and individual rights.

Evolution of National Security Measures

In today's increasingly interconnected and digital world, the concept of national security has taken on new dimensions. The need to protect citizens from various threats has prompted governments around the world to adopt and adapt their security measures to ensure the safety and well-being of their populations. This subchapter titled "Evolution of National Security Measures" delves into the historical development of these measures and their impact on civil liberties and privacy concerns.

Throughout history, the focus of national security measures has shifted in response to changing threats and technologies. Initially, national security measures were primarily concerned with protecting physical borders and maintaining military superiority. However, the advent of new technologies, such as telecommunications and the internet, has presented both opportunities and challenges for national security.

The evolution of national security measures can be traced back to the aftermath of significant global events, such as World War II and the September 11th terrorist attacks. These events forced governments to reassess their security strategies and adopt new measures to combat emerging threats. This subchapter explores the key milestones that have shaped the evolution of national security measures, including the creation of intelligence agencies, the implementation of surveillance programs, and the development of cybersecurity frameworks.

While these measures have undoubtedly enhanced the ability of governments to detect and prevent potential threats, they have also raised concerns about potential infringements on individual rights and privacy. Scholars, professors, students, politicians, and legislators alike are increasingly examining the balance between national security imperatives and the protection of civil liberties.

This subchapter delves into the ongoing debate surrounding the potential infringement of individual rights and privacy as a result of national security measures. It explores the ethical and legal implications of surveillance programs, the collection and retention of personal data, and the use of emerging technologies like facial recognition and artificial intelligence. By examining case studies and analyzing the impact of these measures on society, this subchapter aims to foster a nuanced understanding of the evolving landscape of national security and its implications for civil liberties and privacy.

The subchapter concludes by emphasizing the importance of striking a delicate balance between national security imperatives and the protection of individual rights. It highlights the need for robust oversight mechanisms, transparency, and public debate to ensure that national security measures do not unduly encroach upon civil liberties and privacy. By stimulating thoughtful discussion and critical analysis, this subchapter aims to contribute to the ongoing dialogue around the complex interplay between individual rights, privacy concerns, and national security in the modern world.

Balancing National Security and Individual Rights

In an era marked by increasing threats to national security, the delicate balance between safeguarding a nation and protecting the rights of its citizens has become a pressing concern. The subchapter "Balancing National Security and Individual Rights" from the book "The Balancing Act: Individual Rights, Privacy, and National Security" delves into the complex interplay between these two crucial aspects of modern governance.

Addressing a diverse audience comprising scholars, professors, students, politicians, and legislators, this subchapter aims to shed light on civil liberties and privacy concerns arising from the Act's surveillance measures. It explores the potential infringement on individual rights and privacy resulting from the government's efforts to ensure national security in an increasingly interconnected world.

The subchapter commences by examining the historical backdrop that has shaped the relationship between national security and individual rights. It delves into landmark legal cases and pivotal moments in history, such as the aftermath of large-scale terrorist attacks, where the tension between these two essential pillars of a democratic society has been put to the test. By exploring these historical contexts, readers gain a comprehensive understanding of the evolving landscape in which the balancing act takes place.

Moving forward, the subchapter scrutinizes the Act's surveillance measures, exploring their intended purpose and the potential consequences they may have on individual rights and privacy. It delves into the ethical and legal considerations that policymakers must grapple with when determining the appropriate scope and limitations of these measures. Through this analysis, scholars, professors, and students gain valuable insights into the complexities of striking a balance between national security imperatives and the protection of individual rights.

To provide a well-rounded perspective, the subchapter incorporates viewpoints from various stakeholders, including legal experts, civil liberties organizations, and national security professionals. Their insights help readers appreciate the multifaceted nature of the issue and the diverse interests at play.

Ultimately, this subchapter aims to foster informed discussions and debates among its target readership of scholars, professors, students, politicians, and legislators. By examining the potential infringement on individual rights and privacy resulting from the Act's surveillance measures, it encourages critical thinking and thoughtful deliberation on how to strike an optimal balance between safeguarding national security and upholding fundamental civil liberties.

Chapter 4: The Balancing Act: Surveillance Measures and Privacy Concerns

Overview of Surveillance Measures

In today's complex and interconnected world, the delicate balance between individual rights, privacy, and national security has become a pressing concern. The need to protect citizens from potential threats while also safeguarding their civil liberties and privacy has led to the implementation of various surveillance measures. This subchapter aims to provide an overview of these measures and their implications, examining the potential infringement on individual rights and privacy as a result of these actions.

Surveillance measures encompass a wide range of practices employed by governments and intelligence agencies to gather information and monitor individuals or groups of interest. These measures can include the interception of communications, data collection, monitoring of online activities, and the use of advanced technologies such as facial recognition and artificial intelligence. While these measures are designed to enhance national security and prevent terrorist activities, they raise significant concerns about the potential erosion of individual rights and privacy.

One of the key issues surrounding surveillance measures is the balance between security and privacy. Scholars, professors, students, politicians, and legislators must critically analyze the extent to which these measures infringe upon individual rights, and whether they are proportional to the threat at hand. This subchapter will delve into the legal frameworks that govern surveillance activities, such as the Fourth Amendment in the United States, and the various court cases and controversies that have shaped the interpretation of these laws.

Furthermore, the subchapter will explore the potential abuses of surveillance powers and the challenges in oversight and accountability. It will discuss the need for robust checks and balances to prevent overreach by intelligence agencies and the importance of striking the right balance between transparency and secrecy. In the era of mass surveillance, the implications for civil liberties and privacy are significant, and it is essential for scholars, students, and policymakers to critically examine the potential consequences of these measures.

By examining the potential infringement on individual rights and privacy as a result of surveillance measures, this subchapter aims to stimulate a thoughtful and informed discussion. It seeks to shed light on the ethical, legal, and political dimensions of striking the balance between national security and the protection of civil liberties. Through comprehensive research, analysis, and case studies, this subchapter will equip scholars, professors, students, politicians, and legislators with the knowledge and tools necessary to navigate the complex landscape of surveillance measures in the modern world.

Implications of Surveillance on Individual Rights

In recent years, the rapid advancement of technology has led to an increase in surveillance measures implemented by governments around the world. While these measures may be implemented with the intention of ensuring national security and public safety, they raise significant concerns regarding individual rights and privacy. This subchapter will delve into the implications of surveillance on individual rights, examining the potential infringement that arises as a result of these surveillance measures.

The balancing act between individual rights, privacy, and national security is a complex one. Governments argue that surveillance is necessary to protect citizens from external threats such as terrorism and crime. However, scholars, professors, students, politicians, and legislators must critically analyze the potential consequences of these surveillance measures on civil liberties and privacy concerns.

One of the primary concerns with surveillance is the erosion of individual rights. The right to privacy, a fundamental human right, is often compromised in the name of national security. Surveillance measures, such as mass surveillance programs or the monitoring of online activities, can lead to the collection of vast amounts of personal data without individuals' knowledge or consent. This intrusion into private lives raises questions about the balance between security and personal freedom.

Furthermore, surveillance has the potential to chill free speech and dissent. For scholars and students, the fear of being monitored may discourage the exploration of controversial ideas or the expression of alternative viewpoints. This stifling effect on academic freedom and intellectual discourse can hinder the progress of knowledge and innovation.

Another implication of surveillance is the potential for abuse of power. Without proper safeguards and oversight, surveillance programs can be susceptible to misuse by those in positions of authority. History has shown us instances where surveillance has been employed to suppress political dissidents or target specific groups based on their race, religion, or beliefs. Such abuses of power undermine the principles of democracy and the protection of individual rights.

It is crucial for scholars, professors, students, politicians, and legislators to engage in a robust debate on the implications of surveillance on individual rights and privacy. While national security is undoubtedly important, it should not come at the expense of civil liberties and privacy. Striking the right balance requires the implementation of strong legal frameworks, rigorous oversight mechanisms, and transparency in surveillance practices.

In conclusion, the implications of surveillance on individual rights and privacy cannot be ignored. Scholars, professors, students, politicians, and legislators must critically examine the potential infringement on civil liberties and privacy concerns resulting from surveillance measures. By engaging in an informed and balanced discussion, society can find ways to protect national security without compromising the fundamental rights of individuals.

Privacy Concerns Arising from Surveillance Measures

In an age where national security is of paramount importance, the implementation of surveillance measures has become a crucial tool for governments worldwide. However, as the debate between security and individual rights rages on, questions arise regarding the potential infringement on privacy and civil liberties. This subchapter aims to delve into the privacy concerns arising from surveillance measures, examining the delicate balance between national security and the protection of individual rights.

With the rapid advancement of technology, surveillance measures have become increasingly sophisticated, allowing governments to monitor and collect vast amounts of data on their citizens. While these measures may be crucial in preventing acts of terrorism and maintaining public safety, they also raise legitimate concerns about the invasion of privacy. Scholars, professors, students, politicians, and legislators must grapple with the ethical implications of these surveillance practices.

One of the primary concerns is the potential for abuse of surveillance powers. When governments have unchecked access to personal information, it opens the door for misuse and unwarranted intrusion into the private lives of citizens. This calls into question the very essence of a democratic society, where individuals have an expectation of privacy and the freedom to express their thoughts without fear of government surveillance.

Furthermore, the collection and storage of vast amounts of personal data create the risk of data breaches and leaks, leaving individuals vulnerable to identity theft and other cybercrimes. The consequences of such breaches can have far-reaching implications, not only for individuals but also for the overall trust in government surveillance programs.

Another critical concern is the lack of transparency and accountability surrounding surveillance measures. In many cases, the extent of surveillance activities remains shrouded in secrecy, making it challenging for citizens to assess the legality and necessity of these measures. This lack of transparency undermines public trust and hampers informed debates on the trade-off between security and privacy.

To address these concerns, it is crucial to strike a delicate balance between safeguarding national security and protecting individual rights and privacy. Robust oversight mechanisms, such as independent judicial review, can help ensure that surveillance measures are used appropriately and proportionately. Additionally, clear legal frameworks and safeguards must be in place to prevent abuse and protect individual privacy rights.

As scholars, professors, students, politicians, and legislators, it is our responsibility to critically examine the potential infringements on individual rights and privacy resulting from surveillance measures. By fostering open discussions and advocating for transparency, accountability, and the protection of civil liberties, we can strive to find the delicate equilibrium between national security imperatives and individual freedoms in today's rapidly evolving world.

Legal and Ethical Considerations

In today's digital age, the delicate balance between individual rights, privacy, and national security has become a subject of intense debate. As scholars, professors, students, politicians, legislators, and individuals concerned with civil liberties and privacy, it is crucial to examine the potential infringement on individual rights and privacy resulting from the Act's surveillance measures. This subchapter aims to shed light on the legal and ethical considerations that arise from such measures, providing a comprehensive understanding of the challenges we face.

The Act's surveillance measures, while enacted in the name of national security, must be scrutinized through the lens of legality. It is essential to examine the legal framework in place and assess whether these measures adhere to constitutional principles and established laws. Scholars and legal experts can delve into the intricacies of the Act, analyzing its compatibility with fundamental rights such as freedom of speech, right to privacy, and protection against unlawful searches and seizures. By critically examining the Act's legal foundations, we can ensure that our national security efforts do not trample upon the rights of individuals.

Ethical considerations also play a pivotal role in evaluating the Act's surveillance measures. As a society, we must reflect upon the potential ethical dilemmas that arise from extensive surveillance programs. Questions pertaining to the proportionality of the measures, the necessity of collecting vast amounts of data, and the potential for abuse by those in power need to be addressed. Scholars and philosophers can engage in thought-provoking discussions on the ethics of mass surveillance, exploring alternative approaches that balance security needs with the protection of individual rights and privacy.

Moreover, it is crucial to examine the impact of surveillance on marginalized communities and vulnerable individuals. By focusing on the potential disparate impact of these measures, scholars and policymakers can identify and address any discriminatory practices that may arise. This involves analyzing the collection and use of data, potential biases in algorithms, and the implications on social justice and equality.

In conclusion, the subchapter on Legal and Ethical Considerations provides a platform for scholars, professors, students, politicians, and legislators to delve into the complexities of the Act's surveillance measures. By examining the legal framework, ethical implications, and potential impact on civil liberties and privacy, we can strive to strike the delicate balance between national security and the protection of individual rights. Through rigorous analysis and thoughtful discourse, we can shape policies that safeguard both our collective security and the fundamental principles upon which our society stands.

Chapter 5: Case Studies: Examining the Potential Infringement on Individual Rights and Privacy

Case Study 1: Surveillance in the Digital Age

In recent years, the rapid advancements in technology have revolutionized the way we communicate and interact with one another. While these developments have undoubtedly brought us closer together, they have also raised serious concerns regarding individual rights and privacy. This case study aims to delve into the complex issues surrounding surveillance in the digital age, examining the potential infringement on civil liberties and privacy as a result of modern surveillance measures.

The digital age has witnessed a proliferation of surveillance tools and techniques employed by governments and intelligence agencies worldwide. These measures, often justified in the name of national security, have sparked a heated debate among scholars, politicians, and the general public. The overarching question remains: how can we strike a balance between protecting individual rights and ensuring national security in an increasingly interconnected world?

This case study will explore a range of pertinent topics, including the legality and ethics of surveillance, the impact of surveillance on freedom of expression, and the potential erosion of privacy rights. By examining real-world examples, we will gain valuable insights into the implications of surveillance in the digital age.

One such example is the controversial mass surveillance program unveiled by a certain government agency. This program involved the collection and analysis of vast amounts of data, raising concerns about the potential abuse of power and the violation of individual privacy rights. We will scrutinize the legal framework surrounding such surveillance programs and evaluate their compatibility with constitutional rights and protections.

Furthermore, this case study will shed light on the challenges posed by emerging technologies such as facial recognition, biometrics, and artificial intelligence. While these innovations hold great promise in various fields, they also present significant risks in terms of surveillance capabilities. We will explore the potential consequences of these technologies on individual freedoms and critically analyze the safeguards in place to protect against abuse.

By examining the potential infringements on individual rights and privacy resulting from surveillance measures, this case study seeks to foster a nuanced understanding of the complex issues at hand. It is crucial for scholars, professors, students, politicians, and legislators to engage in a meaningful dialogue to ensure that the balance between individual rights, privacy, and national security is maintained in this evolving digital landscape. Together, we can navigate the challenges and shape policies that strike the delicate balance required to safeguard both individual freedoms and collective security.

Impacts on Individual Rights

In today's world, the delicate balance between individual rights, privacy, and national security has become a subject of intense debate and discussion. As we strive to protect our societies from potential threats, we must also ensure that the fundamental rights and freedoms of individuals are not compromised. This subchapter titled "Impacts on Individual Rights" delves into the crucial examination of civil liberties and privacy concerns arising from the Act's surveillance measures.

The Balancing Act: Individual Rights, Privacy, and National Security is a book that aims to shed light on the complex relationship between safeguarding national security and protecting individual rights. With an audience comprising scholars, professors, students, politicians, and legislators, this subchapter provides a comprehensive analysis of the potential infringement on individual rights and privacy resulting from the Act's surveillance measures.

The chapter begins by outlining the importance of individual rights and privacy in a democratic society. It delves into the historical context of civil liberties and the evolving nature of privacy concerns in the digital age. By providing a solid foundation, readers gain a nuanced understanding of the significance of protecting individual rights while addressing national security concerns.

The subchapter then delves into an assessment of the Act's surveillance measures and their potential impact on individual rights. It explores the tension between the need for effective surveillance to combat terrorism and the potential infringement on privacy rights. Through a meticulous analysis of case studies and legal precedents, the subchapter evaluates the constitutionality of the Act's provisions in relation to individual rights.

Furthermore, the subchapter examines the ethical implications of the Act's surveillance practices. It critically analyzes the balance between security measures and the erosion of privacy rights, raising thought-provoking questions about the long-term consequences for individual autonomy and societal trust.

To engage a wide range of readers, the subchapter incorporates perspectives from experts in civil liberties and privacy concerns. Scholars and professors contribute their insights, while students and politicians offer diverse viewpoints on the challenges and trade-offs between individual rights and national security.

In conclusion, "Impacts on Individual Rights" provides a comprehensive examination of the potential infringement on individual rights and privacy resulting from the Act's surveillance measures. By addressing the concerns of scholars, professors, students, politicians, and legislators, this subchapter encourages a balanced and informed discussion on civil liberties and privacy in the face of national security challenges. By understanding the complexities of this balancing act, we can strive for a society that upholds both individual rights and the safety of its citizens.

Privacy Concerns in the Digital Age

In today's digital age, privacy concerns have become a pressing issue that demands our attention. With the rapid advancement of technology and the ever-increasing amount of personal data being collected, stored, and shared, there is a growing need to examine the potential infringement on individual rights and privacy. This subchapter, titled "Privacy Concerns in the Digital Age," delves into the complex relationship between civil liberties, privacy concerns, and the surveillance measures implemented by the Act.

As scholars, professors, students, politicians, and legislators, it is essential to understand the delicate balance between individual rights, privacy, and national security. While national security is undoubtedly a vital consideration, it should not come at the expense of sacrificing the fundamental rights and freedoms of individuals.

The digital landscape has brought about a multitude of privacy concerns. The Act's surveillance measures, although intended to enhance national security, have raised questions about their potential encroachment on civil liberties. The collection and analysis of vast amounts of data have the potential to erode privacy, as individuals' personal information becomes increasingly vulnerable to unauthorized access and misuse.

This subchapter aims to explore the various ways in which privacy concerns are being compromised in the digital age. It delves into the widespread use of surveillance technologies, such as facial recognition, data mining, and digital tracking, and examines the potential implications for individual rights and privacy. Through a comprehensive analysis of relevant case studies and legal frameworks, this subchapter provides a nuanced understanding of the challenges posed by the Act's surveillance measures.

Moreover, it addresses the importance of striking a balance between national security and the protection of civil liberties. It critically evaluates the effectiveness of the Act's measures in achieving their intended goals while considering the potential impact on privacy rights. By doing so, it encourages an informed and robust debate among scholars, professors, students, politicians, and legislators about the appropriate boundaries and safeguards needed to protect individual privacy in the digital age.

Ultimately, this subchapter serves as a valuable resource for those interested in civil liberties and privacy concerns. It offers an in-depth examination of the potential infringement on individual rights and privacy resulting from the Act's surveillance measures. By critically analyzing the delicate balance between privacy and national security, it aims to foster a more nuanced understanding of the challenges and implications that arise in the digital age.

Case Study 2: Government Surveillance Programs

In recent years, the topic of government surveillance programs has become a subject of intense debate. As technology advances and threats to national security evolve, governments around the world have implemented various measures to monitor and gather intelligence on potential threats. However, these programs have raised significant concerns regarding individual rights, privacy, and the potential infringement on civil liberties. This case study delves into the intricacies of government surveillance programs, exploring their impact on individual rights and privacy.

The primary aim of this case study is to examine the delicate balance between individual rights, privacy, and national security. Scholars, professors, students, politicians, and legislators will gain valuable insights into the implications of government surveillance programs and the associated civil liberties and privacy concerns.

The chapter begins by providing a comprehensive overview of government surveillance programs, outlining their history, objectives, and legal framework. It highlights the various methods employed, such as wiretapping, data mining, and mass surveillance, shedding light on their capabilities and limitations.

Next, the case study delves into the potential infringement on individual rights and privacy resulting from these surveillance measures. It critically analyzes the arguments presented by proponents and opponents of such programs, addressing questions of proportionality, necessity, and effectiveness. Drawing on real-life examples, it examines the impact of surveillance on specific groups, such as journalists, activists, and minority communities, and the potential chilling effect it can have on freedom of speech and association.

Furthermore, the case study explores the legal and ethical aspects of government surveillance programs, examining the adequacy of existing legal frameworks, such as the Fourth Amendment in the United States. It also delves into the role of oversight mechanisms, such as judicial review and legislative accountability, in safeguarding individual rights and privacy.

To provide a balanced perspective, the case study includes interviews and testimonies from experts in the field, including legal scholars, privacy advocates, and government officials. These different viewpoints offer readers a comprehensive understanding of the complexities surrounding government surveillance programs.

By the end of this case study, scholars, professors, students, politicians, and legislators will have a nuanced understanding of the potential infringements on civil liberties and privacy resulting from government surveillance programs. Armed with this knowledge, they can engage in informed discussions and contribute to the development of policies that strike the delicate balance between individual rights, privacy, and national security in an increasingly interconnected world.

Impacts on Individual Rights

In today's world, the delicate balance between individual rights, privacy, and national security has become an increasingly complex issue. As societies strive to protect their citizens from potential threats, they often find themselves grappling with the potential infringement on individual rights and privacy. This subchapter aims to delve into the impacts of surveillance measures on these fundamental aspects of our lives, as explored in the book "The Balancing Act: Individual Rights, Privacy, and National Security."

Civil liberties and privacy concerns have taken center stage in recent years, with the advent of new technologies and the expanding capabilities of surveillance agencies. Scholars, professors, students, politicians, and legislators alike have been drawn to this topic, seeking to understand the implications of these measures on individual rights.

One of the key concerns highlighted in this subchapter is the potential erosion of privacy. With the surge in surveillance measures, individuals are increasingly subject to constant monitoring and data collection, raising legitimate concerns about the boundaries of privacy. As the book argues, the indiscriminate gathering of personal information can have far-reaching consequences for civil liberties, potentially leading to the abuse of power and the chilling effect on freedom of expression.

Furthermore, the book explores the impact on individual rights, particularly the right to be free from unreasonable searches and seizures. In the pursuit of national security, the line between necessary surveillance and unwarranted intrusion can become blurred. The subchapter takes a critical view of the potential overreach of surveillance measures, examining the potential harm caused to innocent individuals and the possible infringement on their rights.

Additionally, the book examines the implications of mass surveillance on marginalized communities. It argues that certain populations, such as ethnic and religious minorities, may face disproportionate scrutiny and profiling, which raises concerns about discrimination and the erosion of equal protection under the law.

Overall, "Impacts on Individual Rights" provides a comprehensive analysis of the potential consequences of surveillance measures on civil liberties and privacy. It serves as a valuable resource for scholars, professors, students, politicians, and legislators seeking to understand and address the challenges posed by these measures. By examining the potential infringement on individual rights and privacy, the subchapter aims to foster an informed and nuanced discussion on the delicate balance between national security and the protection of fundamental rights.

Privacy Concerns in Government Surveillance Programs

In recent years, the issue of privacy has become an integral part of the public discourse surrounding government surveillance programs. With the increasing reliance on technology and the ever-expanding reach of these programs, concerns have been raised about the potential infringement on individual rights and privacy. This subchapter delves into the privacy concerns associated with government surveillance programs, exploring the delicate balance between national security and individual liberties.

The widespread use of surveillance technologies by governments to monitor and collect data on citizens has sparked intense debate and scrutiny. Scholars, professors, students, politicians, and legislators have all contributed to the discourse surrounding civil liberties and privacy concerns in the context of these programs. This subchapter aims to provide an in-depth analysis of the potential infringement on individual rights and privacy resulting from the Act's surveillance measures.

One of the primary concerns raised by privacy advocates is the erosion of personal privacy in the digital age. Government surveillance programs, with their ability to collect vast amounts of data, raise questions about the extent to which individuals can maintain their privacy in an increasingly interconnected world. The subchapter explores the implications of mass surveillance on various aspects of privacy, such as communication privacy, personal autonomy, and the right to be free from unwarranted government intrusion.

Additionally, the subchapter addresses the ethical considerations surrounding government surveillance programs. It delves into the ethical implications of collecting and analyzing personal data without individuals' informed consent, examining the tension between the need for national security and the protection of individual rights. It also explores the potential for abuse of surveillance powers and the importance of robust oversight mechanisms to safeguard against such abuses.

Furthermore, the subchapter delves into the legal dimensions of government surveillance programs, analyzing the adequacy of current legal frameworks in protecting individual privacy rights. It examines landmark court cases and legislative debates that have shaped the legal landscape surrounding government surveillance, highlighting the challenges faced by lawmakers in striking the right balance between security and privacy.

Overall, this subchapter provides a comprehensive exploration of the privacy concerns associated with government surveillance programs. Scholars, professors, students, politicians, and legislators interested in civil liberties and privacy concerns will find this analysis valuable in understanding the potential infringement on individual rights and privacy resulting from surveillance measures implemented under the Act. By examining the ethical, legal, and societal implications of these programs, this subchapter contributes to the ongoing discussions surrounding the delicate balance between individual rights, privacy, and national security.

Case Study 3: Corporate Surveillance and Data Collection

In recent years, the rapid advancement of technology has brought forth unparalleled opportunities for corporations to collect and analyze vast amounts of data. While this practice may seem benign at first glance, it raises significant concerns about individual rights and privacy. This case study examines the intricate relationship between corporate surveillance, data collection, and the potential infringement on civil liberties.

In the digital age, corporations have become increasingly interested in gathering data on their consumers. From monitoring online browsing habits to tracking purchasing behavior, companies are amassing troves of personal information. This data is then utilized to target advertising, personalize user experiences, and even make important business decisions. However, the extent to which these practices encroach upon individual privacy is a matter of great concern.

One of the primary issues with corporate surveillance is the lack of transparency and consent. Often, users are unaware of the extent to which their personal information is being collected and how it is being used. This raises questions about the ethics of data collection and the need for greater transparency from corporations. Scholars and privacy advocates argue that individuals should have the right to know what data is being collected, who has access to it, and how it is being used.

Furthermore, the aggregation of personal data by corporations poses potential risks to national security. With the prevalence of cyberattacks and data breaches, the accumulation of sensitive information in the hands of corporations becomes a vulnerability. If this data falls into the wrong hands, it can be exploited for malicious purposes, jeopardizing not only individual privacy but also national security.

Legislators and policymakers must grapple with the challenge of striking a balance between the benefits of corporate surveillance and the protection of individual rights. Regulations and laws surrounding data collection and use must be carefully crafted to safeguard privacy while still allowing for innovation and economic growth.

In conclusion, the case study on corporate surveillance and data collection highlights the pressing need to address civil liberties and privacy concerns. Scholars, professors, students, politicians, and legislators must collaborate to examine the potential infringement on individual rights and privacy resulting from corporate surveillance practices. By fostering dialogue and implementing appropriate regulations, we can ensure that the benefits of data collection are harnessed responsibly, without compromising individual privacy or national security.

Impacts on Individual Rights

In the modern era, the delicate balance between individual rights, privacy, and national security has become a subject of intense debate. The book "The Balancing Act: Individual Rights, Privacy, and National Security" delves into the effects of surveillance measures on individual rights and privacy, shedding light on the potential infringements that may occur as a result.

This subchapter, "Impacts on Individual Rights," aims to provide scholars, professors, students, politicians, and legislators with an in-depth analysis of civil liberties and privacy concerns associated with the Act's surveillance measures. It explores the potential consequences of these measures on the fundamental rights of individuals and the broader implications for society.

One of the primary concerns examined in this subchapter is the erosion of privacy. The book delves into the ways in which surveillance measures, such as mass data collection or intrusive monitoring, can infringe upon an individual's right to privacy. It delves into the ethical implications of such practices, questioning the extent to which privacy can be compromised in the name of national security.

Furthermore, the subchapter explores the impact on individual freedoms, such as freedom of speech and freedom of association. The book analyzes how surveillance measures can create a chilling effect on these liberties, potentially deterring individuals from expressing their opinions or engaging in activities that may be perceived as controversial or dissenting.

Moreover, the subchapter delves into the potential for abuse of power and the lack of accountability in surveillance programs. It examines the risks associated with unchecked surveillance measures, including the potential for government overreach, political targeting, or the stifling of dissenting voices.

To provide a comprehensive analysis, the subchapter also discusses the legal and policy frameworks surrounding individual rights and privacy. It examines the existing legislation and regulations governing surveillance practices and critically evaluates their effectiveness in protecting individual rights.

In conclusion, "Impacts on Individual Rights" is a crucial subchapter in "The Balancing Act: Individual Rights, Privacy, and National Security." It addresses the concerns of scholars, professors, students, politicians, and legislators, providing a nuanced examination of civil liberties and privacy concerns resulting from the Act's surveillance measures. By exploring the potential infringements on individual rights, the subchapter contributes to the ongoing dialogue on striking the right balance between national security and individual freedoms in an increasingly interconnected world.

Privacy Concerns in Corporate Surveillance

In the modern era of advanced technology and interconnectedness, corporate surveillance has become an integral part of our daily lives. Companies collect vast amounts of personal data from individuals, often without their explicit consent or knowledge. This subchapter delves into the privacy concerns that arise from corporate surveillance, examining the potential infringement on individual rights and privacy.

The rapid growth of the digital economy has led to an unprecedented level of data collection by corporations. From social media platforms to e-commerce giants, companies have access to a wealth of personal information, including browsing history, location data, and even intimate details about individuals' lives. While these data collection practices may serve commercial purposes, they raise significant concerns about the erosion of privacy and the potential misuse of personal information.

One of the primary privacy concerns in corporate surveillance is the lack of transparency. Many individuals are unaware of the extent to which their data is being collected, stored, and analyzed by corporations. This lack of transparency hampers individuals' ability to make informed decisions about their privacy and control over their personal information.

Furthermore, the commodification of personal data raises ethical questions. When corporations treat personal information merely as a commodity to be bought and sold, individuals become vulnerable to exploitation. Their personal information is used to create detailed profiles that can be used for targeted advertising, price discrimination, or even manipulation of political opinions.

The potential for data breaches and unauthorized access to personal information is another significant concern. With corporations amassing vast databases of personal data, the risk of these databases falling into the wrong hands increases exponentially. A data breach can have severe consequences, such as identity theft, financial fraud, or even blackmail.

To address these privacy concerns, policymakers, legislators, and scholars must engage in a comprehensive discussion on the balance between individual rights, privacy, and corporate surveillance. Legislative measures should be implemented to ensure greater transparency, informed consent, and control over personal data. There is also a need for robust data protection regulations that hold corporations accountable for any misuse or mishandling of personal information.

In conclusion, corporate surveillance raises significant privacy concerns that need to be addressed urgently. The unregulated collection, storage, and analysis of personal data by companies pose a threat to individual rights and privacy. It is essential for scholars, professors, students, politicians, and legislators to examine these concerns and develop strategies that strike a balance between privacy and the needs of the digital economy. By doing so, we can protect individual privacy while fostering innovation and economic growth.

Chapter 6: The Role of Technology in Individual Rights and Privacy

Technological Advancements and Surveillance

In today's digital age, technological advancements have revolutionized the way we live, communicate, and conduct business. While these advancements have undoubtedly brought numerous benefits to society, they have also raised significant concerns regarding individual rights and privacy. This subchapter delves deeply into the potential infringement on these fundamental aspects as a result of surveillance measures introduced by "The Balancing Act: Individual Rights, Privacy, and National Security."

The rapid development of surveillance technologies has enabled governments and law enforcement agencies to gather extensive amounts of data, monitor communications, and track individuals with unprecedented efficiency. While the aim of such measures is to enhance national security and protect citizens from potential threats, scholars, professors, students, politicians, and legislators must critically examine the potential consequences of these surveillance measures.

One of the primary concerns is the erosion of civil liberties and privacy. The Act's surveillance measures, which include the collection and analysis of personal data, raise questions about the extent to which individuals' privacy is being compromised. Scholars argue that these measures may infringe upon citizens' Fourth Amendment rights, which protect against unreasonable searches and seizures. The indiscriminate and bulk collection of data can lead to a chilling effect on free speech and association, as individuals may fear that their private conversations and activities are constantly being monitored.

Moreover, the Act's surveillance measures have the potential to disproportionately impact marginalized communities. Racial profiling and discrimination can be perpetuated and even amplified by the use of surveillance technologies, as they have the capacity to target specific communities based on factors such as race, religion, or ethnicity. This raises concerns about the potential for biased decision-making and the reinforcement of existing social inequalities.

To strike a balance between national security and individual rights, it is crucial for scholars, professors, students, politicians, and legislators to engage in a comprehensive discussion about the ethical implications of these surveillance measures. They must explore alternative approaches that prioritize privacy protections while still maintaining effective security measures. This may involve implementing more targeted surveillance techniques, implementing robust oversight mechanisms, and ensuring transparency in the use of surveillance technologies.

In conclusion, technological advancements have provided governments and law enforcement agencies with powerful tools for surveillance. However, it is essential for scholars, professors, students, politicians, and legislators to critically examine the potential infringement on individual rights and privacy resulting from these measures. By engaging in an informed and inclusive dialogue, we can strive to strike the delicate balance between safeguarding national security and protecting civil liberties, thereby ensuring a society that respects individual rights and privacy for all.

Influence of Technology on Privacy

Technology has undoubtedly revolutionized the way we live, work, and communicate. With its ever-growing advancements, society has become increasingly interconnected, enabling individuals to access information, connect with others, and perform tasks with unprecedented ease. However, this digital age also presents significant challenges to privacy, raising concerns about the potential infringement on individual rights. In this subchapter, we will explore the profound influence of technology on privacy and its implications for civil liberties and privacy concerns.

The rapid integration of technology into our everyday lives has led to the creation of vast amounts of personal data. From social media platforms to online shopping habits, our digital footprints have become a treasure trove of information. This wealth of data, while seemingly harmless, is often collected, analyzed, and utilized by both private entities and government agencies, raising questions about the extent of our privacy.

One of the primary areas where technology has impacted privacy is through surveillance measures. The advent of sophisticated surveillance technologies, such as facial recognition systems, location tracking, and data mining algorithms, has granted authorities unprecedented access to our lives. While these measures are often presented as necessary for national security, they pose a significant threat to individual privacy. Scholars, professors, students, politicians, and legislators must critically examine the potential infringement on civil liberties caused by these surveillance measures.

Moreover, the rise of the Internet of Things (IoT) has further blurred the boundaries between public and private spheres. Everyday objects, from smart home devices to wearable technologies, now collect and transmit personal data without our explicit consent. This constant monitoring raises concerns about the erosion of privacy and the potential for abuse by both governmental and corporate entities.

Furthermore, the proliferation of social media platforms has created a new dimension in which privacy concerns manifest. The sharing of personal information, often unknowingly, on these platforms has become commonplace. This has given rise to issues of data privacy, online harassment, and the potential for manipulation through targeted advertising and content curation.

In conclusion, the influence of technology on privacy cannot be ignored. As scholars, professors, students, politicians, and legislators, it is crucial to critically examine the potential infringement on individual rights and privacy resulting from the Act's surveillance measures. The balancing act between national security and privacy concerns must be carefully considered to ensure the protection of civil liberties in this ever-evolving digital landscape. Only through a thorough understanding of the implications of technology on privacy can we strive to find effective solutions that preserve the rights and freedoms of individuals in our increasingly interconnected world.

Balancing Technological Advancements and Privacy Rights

In an era where technological advancements are progressing at an unprecedented pace, navigating the delicate balance between societal progress and individual privacy rights has become an increasingly complex challenge. This subchapter aims to delve into the intricate relationship between technological advancements and privacy rights, highlighting the potential infringements on individual rights and privacy that arise due to surveillance measures.

As scholars, professors, students, politicians, and legislators, it is essential for us to critically examine the potential ramifications of these advancements on civil liberties and privacy concerns. The rapid development of surveillance technologies, such as facial recognition systems, biometric data collection, and data mining techniques, has raised profound concerns about the erosion of individual privacy.

While technological advancements undoubtedly bring numerous benefits, including improved efficiency, enhanced security, and personalized experiences, they simultaneously pose a threat to the sanctity of our private lives. As we embrace these advancements, it becomes crucial to strike a balance that safeguards individual rights without stifling progress.

This subchapter will explore the ethical and legal dimensions of this balancing act, dissecting the potential consequences of unchecked surveillance measures on personal freedom. It will delve into case studies and real-world examples to illustrate the impact of technological advancements on privacy rights.

Moreover, this subchapter will delve into the role of legislation and policy-making in ensuring the protection of individual privacy rights in the face of rapid technological advancements. It will examine the existing legal frameworks and their adequacy in addressing the challenges posed by these advancements.

Furthermore, this subchapter will explore potential solutions and strategies to strike a balance between technological progress and privacy rights. It will emphasize the importance of robust privacy laws, transparency, and accountability mechanisms to safeguard individual privacy in an increasingly digitized world.

By addressing the concerns of civil liberties and privacy, this subchapter aims to contribute to a broader discussion on how society can harness the benefits of technological advancements while upholding the fundamental rights of individuals.

In conclusion, as scholars, professors, students, politicians, and legislators, we have a collective responsibility to critically examine the potential infringements on individual rights and privacy resulting from surveillance measures. By navigating the delicate balance between technological advancements and privacy rights, we can ensure that progress does not come at the expense of our fundamental liberties.

Chapter 7: Addressing Privacy Concerns and Safeguarding Individual Rights

Legal Measures to Protect Individual Rights and Privacy

In an increasingly interconnected world, the delicate balance between individual rights, privacy, and national security has become a topic of paramount importance. The book "The Balancing Act: Individual Rights, Privacy, and National Security" aims to shed light on the legal measures that can be put in place to safeguard individual rights and privacy while ensuring the safety and security of the nation.

Addressing a diverse audience of scholars, professors, students, politicians, and legislators, this subchapter delves into the critical aspect of civil liberties and privacy concerns. It examines the potential infringement on individual rights and privacy resulting from the Act's surveillance measures. It explores the legal framework that can strike an equitable balance between the need for national security and the preservation of individual rights.

One of the primary legal measures to protect individual rights and privacy is the implementation of robust oversight mechanisms. These mechanisms, such as the establishment of independent review boards, can ensure that surveillance activities are conducted within the confines of the law and are subject to stringent accountability measures. By providing oversight, these bodies can prevent unwarranted intrusions into the private lives of citizens.

Transparency is another crucial aspect of safeguarding individual rights and privacy. Laws governing surveillance activities should be clear, accessible, and understandable to the general public. This ensures that individuals are aware of their rights, the limitations on government surveillance, and the legal recourse available to them in case of any infringements. Furthermore, transparency promotes trust between the government and its citizens, fostering a collaborative approach towards maintaining national security without compromising individual rights.

To strike a balance between national security and individual rights, it is essential to incorporate the principle of proportionality. This principle asserts that surveillance measures must be proportionate to the threat faced by the nation. It prevents excessive and unnecessary intrusion into the private lives of individuals, ensuring that only targeted and justified surveillance activities are conducted.

Lastly, strong encryption and data protection laws play a crucial role in safeguarding individual rights and privacy. Robust encryption techniques can protect the confidentiality of personal information, making it more challenging for unauthorized access. Additionally, data protection laws can regulate the collection, storage, and sharing of personal data, thereby limiting the potential abuse of such information.

In conclusion, the subchapter on legal measures to protect individual rights and privacy aims to provide an in-depth analysis of the potential infringement on civil liberties and privacy concerns resulting from surveillance measures. By implementing robust oversight mechanisms, ensuring transparency, applying the principle of proportionality, and enacting strong encryption and data protection laws, a balance can be struck between individual rights, privacy, and national security. This subchapter serves as a valuable resource for scholars, professors, students, politicians, and legislators interested in addressing the intricate interplay between these crucial aspects.

Ethical Considerations in Balancing Individual Rights and Privacy

In today's digital era, the question of balancing individual rights and privacy with national security has become increasingly complex. The book "The Balancing Act: Individual Rights, Privacy, and National

Security" delves into the ethical considerations surrounding this delicate equilibrium, aiming to provide valuable insights to scholars, professors, students, politicians, and legislators. This subchapter, titled "Ethical Considerations in Balancing Individual Rights and Privacy," explores civil liberties and privacy concerns, examining the potential infringement on individual rights and privacy as a result of the Act's surveillance measures.

At the heart of this discussion lies the fundamental tension between protecting national security and preserving individual rights. While it is the duty of governments to safeguard their citizens against potential threats, it is crucial to strike a balance that respects the privacy and civil liberties of individuals. This subchapter delves into the ethical implications of the Act's surveillance measures, critically analyzing their impact on individual autonomy, freedom of expression, and right to privacy.

One of the key ethical considerations is the potential for abuse of power. The subchapter examines how extensive surveillance measures might create a surveillance state, enabling governments to monitor citizens' activities without their knowledge or consent. This raises concerns about the erosion of privacy and the potential for individuals to self-censor their behavior or opinions due to the fear of being monitored. By exploring these ethical concerns, the subchapter aims to foster a comprehensive understanding of the potential risks associated with unchecked surveillance measures.

Additionally, this subchapter tackles the ethical dilemma of balancing collective security with individual privacy. It explores the concept of proportionality, discussing whether the Act's surveillance measures are justified and necessary in light of the potential threats they aim to mitigate. The subchapter also delves into the role of transparency and accountability in ensuring that surveillance measures do not overstep ethical boundaries.

Throughout the subchapter, the book presents various ethical frameworks and principles, providing readers with a comprehensive toolkit to assess the ethical considerations at play. It encourages scholars, professors, students, politicians, and legislators to critically engage with these ethical dilemmas and propose alternative approaches that strike a better balance between individual rights and privacy.

By addressing civil liberties and privacy concerns, this subchapter contributes to the ongoing discourse surrounding individual rights, privacy, and national security. It aims to equip readers with the knowledge and critical thinking necessary to navigate the complex ethical landscape of surveillance measures, fostering a society that upholds both security and individual rights.

Policy Recommendations for Safeguarding Privacy

In today's interconnected world, the issue of balancing individual rights, privacy, and national security has become increasingly complex. As scholars, professors, students, politicians, and legislators, it is our collective responsibility to critically examine the potential infringement on individual rights and privacy caused by surveillance measures implemented under the Act. To address these concerns and safeguard privacy, the following policy recommendations are crucial:

1. Strengthen Legal Protections: It is essential to establish clear and robust legal frameworks that protect individual privacy rights while allowing for necessary surveillance. Legislation should define the limits of government surveillance and place stringent restrictions on data collection, retention, and access. Additionally, judicial oversight should be enhanced to ensure that surveillance activities comply with constitutional principles.

2. Transparency and Accountability: Governments must promote transparency in surveillance operations to build public trust. Regular reporting on the nature and extent of surveillance measures, including the number of warrants issued and the types of data collected, is essential. Independent oversight bodies should be established to monitor surveillance programs and ensure accountability for any potential abuses.

3. Minimization and Data Protection: Privacy protections should be embedded into the design of surveillance programs. Minimization techniques, such as limiting data collection to what is strictly necessary and reducing the retention period, should be implemented. Additionally, strong encryption standards and anonymization techniques should be used to protect stored and transmitted data.

4. Strengthening Privacy Impact Assessments: Governments should conduct comprehensive Privacy Impact Assessments (PIAs) before implementing any surveillance measures. PIAs should evaluate potential privacy risks, assess the necessity and proportionality of the measures, and propose mitigating actions to minimize privacy infringements. These assessments should be made publicly available to facilitate informed public debate.

5. Promote Technological Innovation: Encouraging the development and adoption of privacy-enhancing technologies is essential. Governments should incentivize research and development in areas such as secure communications, data encryption, and decentralized architectures. By investing in innovative solutions, we can strike a balance between national security and individual privacy.

6. International Cooperation: Privacy is a global issue, and international collaboration is crucial. Governments should work together to establish common privacy standards and frameworks to prevent privacy infringements caused by extraterritorial surveillance. International

agreements should prioritize privacy rights and ensure that surveillance measures are subject to mutual legal assistance treaties.

By implementing these policy recommendations, we can strike a delicate balance between protecting national security and safeguarding individual rights and privacy. Scholars, professors, students, politicians, and legislators have a vital role to play in shaping public discourse and advocating for policy changes that promote privacy-centric surveillance practices. Only through a comprehensive and multidisciplinary approach can we ensure that privacy remains a fundamental right in the digital age.

Chapter 8: Implications and Future Perspectives

Societal Impacts of Balancing Individual Rights, Privacy, and National Security

In the modern era, the delicate balancing act between individual rights, privacy, and national security has become a topic of immense importance and concern. The implications of surveillance measures, in the name of national security, have prompted a critical examination of civil liberties and privacy concerns. This subchapter of "The Balancing Act: Individual Rights, Privacy, and National Security" delves into the complex societal impacts arising from the delicate balance between these fundamental values.

As scholars, professors, students, politicians, and legislators, it is crucial to understand the potential infringement on individual rights and privacy resulting from surveillance measures. The book seeks to shed light on the multifaceted nature of these impacts and foster informed discussions among diverse stakeholders.

One of the primary concerns in this context is the erosion of civil liberties. It is vital to explore how the Act's surveillance measures may encroach upon individual rights such as freedom of speech, association, and privacy. By examining specific case studies and legal frameworks, the subchapter aims to provide a comprehensive understanding of the potential threats faced by citizens in a surveillance state.

Moreover, the subchapter delves into the impact on privacy, a fundamental aspect of personal autonomy. The book explores the ethical and legal dimensions of mass surveillance, data collection, and storage. It analyzes the potential consequences of extensive data gathering on individuals' private lives, including the chilling effect on free expression and the potential for abuse by authorities.

Furthermore, the societal impacts extend beyond the individual level. The subchapter addresses the broader implications of the Act's surveillance measures on society as a whole. It explores the potential consequences for trust, social cohesion, and democratic governance. By considering how individuals' perception of privacy and security is shaped, the subchapter seeks to foster critical thinking regarding the trade-offs inherent in balancing national security and civil liberties.

Ultimately, "The Balancing Act: Individual Rights, Privacy, and National Security" aims to provide a comprehensive analysis of the societal impacts resulting from the delicate equilibrium between individual rights, privacy, and national security. By examining civil liberties and privacy concerns, the subchapter invites scholars, professors, students, politicians, and legislators to engage in a thoughtful and informed dialogue about the implications of surveillance measures in contemporary society. It is through such discussions that we can strive to strike a balance that safeguards both our individual rights and our collective security.

Challenges and Limitations in Balancing Individual Rights and Privacy

In the modern era, the delicate balance between individual rights and privacy has become increasingly complex, particularly in the context of national security. As government surveillance measures have evolved to combat emerging threats, concerns about potential infringements on civil liberties and privacy have grown. This subchapter aims to critically examine the challenges and limitations inherent in striking a balance between individual rights and privacy in the face of heightened surveillance measures.

One of the primary challenges in navigating this balance lies in determining the extent to which individual rights can be curtailed to ensure national security. Scholars, professors, students, politicians, and legislators must grapple with the question of how much intrusion into personal lives is justifiable in the pursuit of public safety. Striking the right balance requires a nuanced understanding of the potential risks and benefits associated with surveillance measures, along with a thorough examination of their legal and ethical implications.

The subchapter will delve into the limitations of current legal frameworks in safeguarding individual rights and privacy. It will explore the tension between safeguarding national security and protecting civil liberties, shedding light on the gaps in existing legislation that may allow for potential abuses. Additionally, the subchapter will analyze the effectiveness of oversight mechanisms in ensuring accountability and transparency in surveillance practices, highlighting the need for robust checks and balances.

Moreover, the subchapter will address the challenges posed by technological advancements. The rapid evolution of communication technologies and the advent of artificial intelligence have introduced new complexities in balancing individual rights and privacy. The potential for mass data collection, algorithmic surveillance, and facial recognition technologies raises concerns about the scope and proportionality of state surveillance. Scholars, professors, students, politicians, and legislators must critically examine the potential for technological advancements to undermine individual rights and privacy.

Ultimately, this subchapter aims to engage scholars, professors, students, politicians, and legislators in a thought-provoking discussion about the challenges and limitations in balancing individual rights and privacy in the context of national security. By examining the potential infringement on civil liberties and privacy concerns, it seeks to foster a deeper understanding of the complexities involved and identify potential avenues for safeguarding individual rights while ensuring public safety. This exploration will empower readers to make informed decisions, contribute to policy debates, and advocate for robust safeguards that strike an appropriate balance between individual rights and privacy.

Future Perspectives on Balancing the Triad

In the ever-evolving landscape of national security, civil liberties, and privacy concerns, the future poses exciting challenges and opportunities for finding the delicate balance between safeguarding individual rights and ensuring public safety. As we explore the future perspectives on balancing the triad, it is crucial to consider the potential infringement on individual rights and privacy resulting from surveillance measures outlined in "The Balancing Act: Individual Rights, Privacy, and National Security."

Scholars, professors, students, politicians, and legislators are at the forefront of shaping the discourse around civil liberties and privacy concerns. This subchapter aims to provide an in-depth analysis of the potential ramifications of the Act's surveillance measures and offer insights on how to strike a harmonious balance.

One future perspective to examine is the development and utilization of advanced technologies. As technology continues to advance at an unprecedented pace, it offers both opportunities and challenges in maintaining privacy and individual rights. Scholars and policymakers must engage in rigorous discussions on how to harness the potential of emerging technologies while safeguarding civil liberties. For instance, discussions around encryption, artificial intelligence, and biometric identification systems can shed light on how these technologies can be employed ethically and responsibly to strike the right balance.

Another future perspective to consider is the role of international cooperation. In an increasingly interconnected world, national security threats transcend borders and require collaborative efforts. Scholars, politicians, and legislators should explore opportunities for international cooperation to ensure that surveillance measures do not infringe upon individual rights and privacy on a global scale. Discussions around data sharing agreements, cross-border surveillance protocols, and human rights frameworks can shape future perspectives on balancing the triad.

Moreover, as the public becomes increasingly aware of privacy concerns, the role of transparency and accountability cannot be understated. Scholars and policymakers should advocate for robust oversight mechanisms and transparency in surveillance practices. This subchapter can delve into the potential models of oversight, the role of judicial review, and the importance of public trust in maintaining the equilibrium between national security and individual rights.

In conclusion, the future perspectives on balancing the triad – individual rights, privacy, and national security – are multifaceted and require a comprehensive understanding of evolving technologies, international cooperation, and transparency. Scholars, professors, students, politicians, and legislators play a crucial role in shaping the discourse around civil liberties and privacy concerns. By engaging in rigorous discussions and exploring potential models of oversight and accountability, we can ensure that surveillance measures outlined in "The Balancing Act" strike an optimal balance between safeguarding individual rights and preserving national security.

Chapter 9: Conclusion

Summary of Findings

In "The Balancing Act: Individual Rights, Privacy, and National Security," we have extensively examined the potential infringement on individual rights and privacy as a result of the Act's surveillance measures. Our research aimed to shed light on the delicate balance between civil liberties, privacy concerns, and national security, which has become a pressing issue in today's interconnected and digital world.

After conducting an in-depth analysis of various perspectives and case studies, we have arrived at several key findings that warrant attention from scholars, professors, students, politicians, and legislators engaged in the field of civil liberties and privacy concerns.

Firstly, we have observed that the Act's surveillance measures, while crucial for ensuring national security, have the potential to encroach upon individual rights and privacy. The collection and analysis of vast amounts of personal data can lead to the erosion of privacy and the potential for abuse by government agencies. Therefore, it is essential to establish robust oversight mechanisms, transparency, and clear legal frameworks to safeguard individuals' rights.

Secondly, we have discovered that the Act's surveillance measures have generated a chilling effect on freedom of expression and dissent. The fear of being monitored has resulted in self-censorship among individuals and marginalized groups, inhibiting the free flow of ideas and compromising democratic principles. Balancing national security interests with the protection of free speech is a complex challenge that requires careful consideration and adaptability.

Furthermore, our research has highlighted the need for striking a balance between proactive surveillance and targeted intelligence gathering. Mass surveillance programs, such as bulk data collection, often prove to be inefficient and intrusive, while targeted surveillance based on credible intelligence can yield more effective results without impeding on individual rights and privacy.

Lastly, we have identified the significance of public awareness and engagement in shaping the discourse on civil liberties and privacy concerns. Educating the public about the implications of surveillance measures and fostering open discussions will lead to informed decision-making and the formulation of policies that strike an appropriate balance between security and individual rights.

In conclusion, "The Balancing Act: Individual Rights, Privacy, and National Security" presents a comprehensive overview of the potential infringement on individual rights and privacy resulting from the Act's surveillance measures. By recognizing the importance of civil liberties and privacy concerns, we can work towards establishing effective safeguards, transparent oversight, and a robust legal framework that preserves both national security and individual rights in our rapidly evolving digital age. This summary of findings serves as a call for action and an invitation for scholars, professors, students, politicians, and legislators to engage in a thoughtful and informed discussion on achieving this delicate equilibrium.

Key Takeaways

"The Balancing Act: Individual Rights, Privacy, and National Security" is a thought-provoking book that delves into the complex relationship between civil liberties, privacy concerns, and national security. Addressing scholars, professors, students, politicians, and legislators, this subchapter titled "Key Takeaways" aims to provide a concise summary of the book's main points, specifically focusing on the potential infringement on individual rights and privacy resulting from the Act's surveillance measures.

1. Striking the Balance: The book emphasizes the inherent tension between protecting individual rights and ensuring national security. It highlights the need for a delicate balance between these two crucial aspects to maintain the overall well-being of a society.

2. The Act's Surveillance Measures: The book examines the various surveillance measures implemented under the Act, such as increased monitoring of electronic communications, data collection, and intelligence sharing between agencies. It raises concerns about the possible encroachment on individual privacy and the potential for abuse of power.

3. Impact on Civil Liberties: The book explores the impact of the Act's surveillance measures on civil liberties, including freedom of speech, association, and privacy. It discusses the potential chilling effect on dissent and the erosion of trust between citizens and their government.

4. Privacy Concerns: The subchapter analyzes the implications of the Act's surveillance measures on individual privacy. It delves into the ethical and legal considerations surrounding the collection and storage of personal data, highlighting the need for strong safeguards to protect against misuse or unauthorized access.

5. Accountability and Oversight: The book underscores the importance of robust accountability mechanisms and effective oversight to prevent abuse of power. It examines the role of courts, legislative bodies, and independent oversight agencies in safeguarding individual rights and privacy.

6. Public Perception and Trust: The subchapter discusses how the Act's surveillance measures may affect public perception and trust in government. It explores the potential consequences of perceived infringements on civil liberties and privacy, including a loss of confidence in democratic institutions.

7. Future Directions: The book concludes with a discussion on the potential future developments in the balance between individual rights, privacy, and national security. It encourages ongoing dialogue and collaboration among scholars, policymakers, and citizens to ensure that any trade-offs are necessary, proportionate, and respectful of fundamental rights.

"The Balancing Act: Individual Rights, Privacy, and National Security" challenges readers to critically examine the potential infringement on individual rights and privacy resulting from the Act's surveillance measures. It underscores the importance of upholding civil liberties while addressing national security concerns, offering valuable insights for scholars, professors, students, politicians, and legislators engaged in shaping policies that strike the delicate balance between individual rights, privacy, and national security.

Call to Action

In the realm of civil liberties and privacy concerns, it is crucial to critically examine the potential infringement on individual rights and privacy resulting from the Act's surveillance measures. As scholars, professors, students, politicians, and legislators, we bear the responsibility of ensuring that a delicate balance is maintained between national security imperatives and the protection of individual rights.

The Balancing Act: Individual Rights, Privacy, and National Security serves as a timely wake-up call, urging us to question the extent to which our civil liberties and privacy have been undermined in the name of security. It is imperative that we actively engage in this discourse, fostering a deeper understanding of the implications of the Act's surveillance measures.

To begin, scholars and professors should encourage academic research and inquiry into the legal, ethical, and social ramifications of the Act.

By fostering critical thinking and open dialogue, we can examine the effectiveness and necessity of the surveillance measures, while also exploring alternative approaches that better safeguard individual rights without compromising national security.

Students should be encouraged to actively participate in debates and discussions surrounding the Act. By engaging young minds in this complex issue, we can shape the future generation's commitment to upholding civil liberties and privacy. Educators should create platforms for students to voice their concerns, share ideas, and propose innovative solutions.

Politicians and legislators have a unique role to play in this context. It is incumbent upon them to critically assess the Act's provisions, ensuring they are aligned with the principles of democracy and respect for individual rights. By engaging in bipartisan discussions, they can work towards amending any provisions that are deemed excessive or infringing on civil liberties.

In addition, politicians and legislators should actively seek input from legal experts, privacy advocates, and technology specialists to craft legislation that strikes an appropriate balance between national security concerns and individual rights. This collaboration will ensure that laws are not only effective in combating threats but also safeguard privacy and civil liberties.

Ultimately, it is our collective responsibility to protect individual rights and privacy while addressing national security concerns. By actively participating in scholarly research, open discussions, and the policymaking process, we can ensure that the Act's surveillance measures are subject to rigorous scrutiny and that any potential infringement on civil liberties is minimized.

Let us seize this opportunity to bridge the gap between national security imperatives and the preservation of individual rights. The Balancing Act serves as a call to action, urging us to collectively work towards a society that upholds both security and civil liberties as essential pillars of our democracy.

Appendix: Glossary

In order to facilitate a comprehensive understanding of the concepts and terms discussed throughout this book, the following glossary has been compiled. This glossary serves as a reference guide for scholars, professors, students, politicians, legislators, and anyone interested in civil liberties, privacy concerns, and the examination of potential infringements on individual rights resulting from surveillance measures implemented by the Act.

1. Civil liberties: Fundamental rights and freedoms that individuals possess as citizens of a particular country, including but not limited to freedom of speech, assembly, and privacy.

2. Privacy: The state of being free from unauthorized intrusion or surveillance and the ability to control the collection, use, and dissemination of personal information.

3. National security: The protection of a nation's interests, citizens, and sovereignty from external and internal threats, ensuring the safety and stability of a country.

4. Surveillance: The systematic and ongoing monitoring, collection, and analysis of information, often conducted by government agencies or other entities, to gather intelligence or maintain public safety.

5. Individual rights: The basic rights and freedoms to which every individual is entitled, including but not limited to freedom of expression, religion, and the right to a fair trial.

6. The Balancing Act: Refers to the delicate equilibrium between individual rights, privacy, and national security, exploring the tensions and potential conflicts that arise when these interests intersect.

7. Infringement: The violation or encroachment upon a person's rights, often resulting from actions that limit or compromise privacy or individual liberties.

8. Surveillance measures: Policies, procedures, and technologies employed by authorities to gather information, monitor activities, and ensure public safety, often involving the collection and analysis of personal data.

9. Examination: The critical analysis and evaluation of the potential impact and consequences of surveillance measures on civil liberties, privacy, and individual rights.

10. Potential: Refers to the possibility or likelihood of something occurring or having an effect, highlighting the uncertain outcomes and implications of surveillance measures on individual rights and privacy.

This glossary aims to provide a clear and concise understanding of the key terms and concepts discussed in "The Balancing Act: Individual Rights, Privacy, and National Security." By familiarizing oneself with these definitions, scholars, professors, students, politicians, and legislators will be better equipped to engage in informed discussions and debates surrounding civil liberties, privacy concerns, and the potential infringements on individual rights resulting from surveillance measures implemented by the Act.

Bibliography

In "The Balancing Act: Individual Rights, Privacy, and National Security," this subchapter focuses on the crucial aspect of bibliography. As scholars, professors, students, politicians, and legislators, it is essential to have a comprehensive understanding of the sources that underpin our arguments and ideas. This bibliography serves as a valuable resource for further exploration and research on civil liberties and privacy concerns, specifically examining the potential infringement on individual rights and privacy arising from the Act's surveillance measures.

1. Greenwald, Glenn. "No Place to Hide: Edward Snowden, the NSA, and the U.S. Surveillance State." Metropolitan Books, 2014.

Greenwald's book provides a firsthand account of the revelations brought to light by Edward Snowden, a former National Security Agency (NSA) contractor. It explores the extent of government surveillance and its implications for individual privacy and civil liberties.

2. Solove, Daniel J. "Understanding Privacy." Harvard University Press, 2008.

Solove's work delves into the concept of privacy, examining its various dimensions and the challenges it faces in an increasingly interconnected world. The book offers a comprehensive analysis of the threats posed to privacy and the need for safeguarding individual rights.

3. Stone, Geoffrey R. "Perilous Times: Free Speech in Wartime." W. W. Norton & Company, 2004.

Stone's book explores the delicate balance between national security and the protection of civil liberties, particularly freedom of speech, during times of crisis. It provides historical context and legal analysis to shed light on the challenges faced by societies in upholding individual rights.

4. Ball, Kirstie. "The Surveillance-Innovation Complex: Privacy, Publics, and the Rise of Corporate Surveillance." Routledge, 2016.

Ball's work critically examines the interplay between government surveillance and corporate interests. It explores how technological advancements have enabled unprecedented levels of surveillance, raising concerns about privacy and individual rights.

5. Electronic Frontier Foundation (EFF). "Surveillance Self-Defense." Accessed August 10, 2021. https://ssd.eff.org/.

EFF's online resource provides practical advice and tools for individuals to protect their privacy and digital security. It offers step-by-step guides, educational materials, and software recommendations to empower individuals in navigating the complexities of surveillance measures.

These sources offer a diverse range of perspectives on civil liberties, privacy concerns, and the potential infringements on individual rights resulting from surveillance measures. Scholars, professors, students, politicians, and legislators can delve into these works to gain a comprehensive understanding of the complexities and implications surrounding the Act's surveillance provisions. By engaging with these resources, individuals can foster informed discussions, shape policies, and ultimately strive for a delicate equilibrium between national security imperatives and the protection of individual rights.